I0141665

NERVOUS READER

SELECTED POETRY by JASON GOODMAN
Second Edition

Copyright c. 1992, 2013
by Jason Goodman
ALL RIGHTS RESERVED
Library of Congress Control
Number: 2013907694
ISBN # 978-0-615-80658-7
Printed in the United States of America
Also by the Author:
A PUZZLED EXISTENCE c. 2011
Library of Congress Control
Number: 2013907693
SIMPLE REFLECTIONS-on a frozen surface
c. 1979
 NERVOUS READER c. 1992
No part of this publication may be reproduced or
transmitted in any form, electronic, mechanical,
photocopy, text, recording or any information
storage & retrieval system without written and
documented permission of the publisher.

Published by:
Alchemy Studio LLc
11 East Lincoln Avenue
Lititz, Pa 17543-1122
Additional title information may be obtained
from our website:
http//www.alchemystudioinc.com

Dedication

"…an I don't look at no goils,"

PROLOGUE

Jason began writing poetry at an early age, his first published book came in 1979, though before that occurred, he was a coffee house reader.

In the late 60's, Jason stepped onto the scene when he read poetry prior to Archibald MacLeish at a local University. He was unaware of who MacLeish was at the time, but after he read, Mr. MacLeish approached him and said "I like your work, it made me laugh, stay at it boy you might have a future, now I have to pay the rent!" He then assumed the stage, something Jason would do for many years to come.

In those days, a coffee shop was your morning stop going to work. But a "coffeehouse", was where the' beats' could be found at night: dark, smoky hidden little holes that someone had to take you to. They had coffee but there was also a stage and an 'open mike' and usually a black stool set in a back corner. You could buy the herb there, if you knew who to ask. Hot jazz, then people like Dylan, that stool was the seat of some of the best. These were the places Jason read his poetry, accompanied by a flute or bongos, someone in his 'groove' picking up his vibes, here were the critics, or his accolades. Jason read everywhere, from the New York

Poetry Society located in Manhattan, to the Crystal Café in Melbourne, Australia. He read by invitation at many colleges and universities, as a favor at Endicott in Salem, Mass. and with Allen Ginsberg as part of a workshop at the University of Colorado in Boulder.

Jason wrote and produced a very successful "event" centered on poetry called "Mental Perspectives", which ran for two sold out nights at College Misericordia, Dallas, Pa. During this time countless books and anthologies published his work, winning first place to honorable mention.

In 1992 Jason published NERVOUS READER. It was a success from the start, selling in bookstores all over the US. But due to his art career, combined with medical issues, he never followed with a second edition until now. While moving recently, Jason's wife found a journal of poetry from the same time period. Here is a new volume of work from the 'beat' generation, timeless poetry that came from the pen of one man, deep insights as valid today and spoken just yesterday. Welcome to the work of a NERVOUS READER.

CHAPTER ONE

Screw you,

Said the screwdriver

to the screw.

The pliers and wrench just smiled,

this was their only child.

Twirling themselves dizzy

until they fall down,

laughing hysterically

while people

cover their eyes.

The sky

near weeping,

little ballerinas

leaping.

Spinning about the ground

until the tears,

and they were gone.

We are John Wayne

drinkin' beer

talking brave

trying to evade

the corrosive feeling

of death.

Alone,

at the front,

waiting for the war

to breathe,

no one there

nobody to impress

no one

to take our place.

One thing remains

our perspiring forehead

of fear.

Medieval iron

slowly turns,

casted weights

internal springs

grotesque figures

with frozen eyes

raise hammers

and soon the sky

cracks open,

another hour

in Cologne

Heat

then darkness,

a faint buzz

in the quiet,

soon the lump appears

followed by an itch,

was it God's intention

the mosquito?

Never cared much for sandals

following Virgil

using hot stones for handles,

deeper we descend

beyond gnashing teeth

screaming

and burning genitalia.

Deeper we go

the stones get cold

sweat pours from my head,

bugs never bite the gun

though my soul grows colder

the deeper we descend

into this hell

called Vietnam!

Cowboy

real man,

Wrangler jacket

shit on his pants.

Horse and camper

Jeep,

four wheel drive,

though at the bar

you look misplaced

disco motif

a guy named Biff,

no shoot-outs here

just Rusty Nails

and a men's room

with soap on the floor

not by accident

I could extend myself

to be more of a man

with a used Corvette

or a few chrome hubcaps.

I could make a statement

about my identity

with a loud muffler

or a pull tab chain,

love me baby

love me

Leaning on the evenings edge

presenting a perfect picture of

vagrancy,

matching the Moons' galvanized sigh

while night

becomes a corner hangout

for metered love.

She runs out after the climax

to insert a quarter,

protection from a ticket

or an early demise.

Her husband comes home at nine

though,

he never was the type

who rode menstrual cycles

run hard and put away wet

Oh! gosh,

a row of phallic symbols

lined so meticulously

on your window sill,

you must be Virgo

studying ceramics

Fookin' bills,

most of the time I ignore

my mail box.

Only the lure of a love letter

draws me near,

I sneak up sniffing the area,

fookin' gas company

brought out Machiavelli,

now I must pay for both gas

and being a fool

Picasso probably knew mayonnaise

though he never admitted it,

I talk to my little red friends

and they tell me things,

secret obsessions.

Apart from the norm

these truths are still valid

in the essence of shadows

cast by filthy French windows

and opaque idealism,

Picasso was a shifty one

flowing into your studio

memorizing colors

absorbing your palette

into New York with Cubism,

before you get there

with a signed contract!

20

The nuns taught me to read

somewhat nervously,

academic Latin

served on starched paper breasts.

A tongue shoveled the altar

with perfect rhythm

soon followed

by a devotion of false truths.

We ate education with a cane

digesting ideas in pain

never interrupting our merciful

instructors,

being excommunicated

while seeking contrition

for having glanced at Darwin's

Origin of the Species

I have been at low tide before

remembering the smell

of fish

swimming on their backs;

pipes and rocks are still exposed

while the beach lies nude.

I have been at low tide alone

or in a fog horns moan

counting a bridge's barnacles

checking the cracks

in a decadent sea wall.

This low tide existence

of crumpled cigarette packs

A coffee ringed Formica countertop

with constant exposure

to the sea of anticipation.

A transistor radio

tries desperately,

a pinochle game

goes on tirelessly,

the green walls

take it in

and grin.

The 'no smoking' sign exists

while the smoke persists

giving the air

a poolroom density

with equal time

to sheets, socks and day old Lo Mein,

without money nothing gets laid!

My refrigerator vegetable bin

is packed with long varieties,

some are peeled while others

are left long and bumpy,

maybe I have been neglecting

something?

The bedspread looks like a salad

and I find spent zucchini

in the bathroom,

what does this it all mean?

Maybe I should give up poetry

and study gourmet cooking?

Thermo Nuclear

Triangles drop

a constant rain,

arrows point

much in vain,

objects fall

one by one,

molecules remain

quite undone,

repulsive

angry

trying desperately

to reach the place

we all succumb

The Sun sets

with three cigarettes

while a nervous sky

reflects Zippo fears,

I walk inside

to be digested

by a parasitical feeling,

knowing night

and not myself

Chandeliers of Styrofoam

hang from the shelves

neon pronounced prisms

accentuate the sale items

of blushing realism,

a pink old man

bags my escape in brown

his glance packaged my intent

with Baptist confirmation,

the clock smiled in silkscreen

so I left,

enlightened

7-11 Zen

for another evening

A Greek chorus

standing within this room,

singing long

their monotonous tune,

moaning notes without end

mainly in the wrong key,

at this ill harmony

steam radiators protest

adding their voice

to cover the sound

of leather soles

scuffing the steps,

bed spring serenade

and toilet flush.

The concert of night

entertaining until light

stealing the silence of

another boring love

The book recites its message

I try very hard

but still feign interest,

words and sentences

seem so distant

so much apart

from the feelings within.

Where is the logic now?

Psychology has abandoned me

all of the philosophies

dreams

plans

have melted away.

The book recites its message

an empty passage

with shallow perception

Tide

Her love

a dream without fantasy

her kiss

a scheme to destroy me.

Her hug

an elephant stampede

her bed

a Dead Sea brought to life,

a volcano without pride

her love

the tide

The bowl cleansed itself

while I tried vainly

to distinguish myself

from the other images

in the mirror.

I noticed a close relationship

between urinals

and a baptismal,

the door opened

with a knocking pipe

and the entire idea

dissipated in a towel

CHAPTER TWO

Greeting's from Vietnam

A table with Salems

Zippo fuel and peanut shells,

a paper with instructions

information and some help.

A cup of ice, leaking on the side

dumped from an ashtray.

My stomach hanging

limply on my belt

my mind creating a splendid

atmosphere

my soul demonstrating

against being here,

unanswered questions

always the same reaction

why?

Some books haven't bindings

they are loose

like paperbacks

broken by age

on a night stand of darkness,

separated chapters

with little blue inserts

or quaint

baby talk messages,

scribbled notes

say I remember my life

everyone's personal essay

within the cardboard vice

stories train

for the contest of life,

not quite novels

mere memoirs,

almost a short story.

"Please step back on the platform

lady,

yes, yes, the main concourse is

that way….."

Buddy, why don't you give up,

for Christ sake

you've been waiting a year!

The laundromat ticks

with a funny noise

scent of soap powder

disgruntled employees,

tee-shirts shrink

dryers spin

quarters drop

kids slobber on their mothers

breasts,

I think of nudist colonies

no laundromat there

simply combed pubic hair

and a gracious smile,

a beer belly flops

buttocks drop

men slobber on themselves

in artificial vanilla flavoring

Banos

Is life a urinal

lined with sharpshooters,

or a commode

with the final say?

Cigarette butts

blown away!

Put on those edible clothes

steeped in sweet ceremonials

I won't tell of the ritual

underneath.

Walk way up there

on those ankle elevators

I will supply tampax

for your nose bleed

Treat

A gigantic butterscotch lifesaver

tis that sun

dissolving slowly

in the ocean,

making waves sweet

and leaving the sky

smackin' its lips

mon!

That claw-hammer

sittin' at the bar havin'

a pint with the carpenter.

Ee's his best friend alright

always hittin' things on the head

either cutting em up

er drivin em in

Hamburger smoke grease

tangled hair falling in lumps,

a sweating brow asks how many,

I reply with cheese.

Evening meal

nothing fried

blood vessels pop

periodically in my eyes

probably from staring

at the grill

or fat filled cleavage

of her business

The wing tip

and sneaker

chase each other

around the room

like two buffoons

the sneaker needs money

and the wing tip smells

marijuana

within the dormitory

rooms

Willy just stood there

carving his name

into the wall,

W-I-L-L-Y

I said, hey Willy

and he said something

in farts and burps,

this is university

and Willy is Pre-Med

or political science

Super studs

are very fast,

sun-tan Mustang

condom Corvette,

super men

orange wheels

magenta tarmac

chrome plated

admirer

Songs and coffee mugs

tap their toes on the rungs

of red fake leather stools

just a mild murmur

through the window,

trucks ready to roll.

Red faced flannel shirts

sip and smoke

hiss and hoot

air brake conversation,

trucks ready to go

hauling the worlds

provisions

Buddha was here earlier

and so was Jesus,

they had a fight.

Buddha walked away

because he is a man,

Jesus was carried off

he is an astronaut

Tonight is

tomorrow's garbage,

squeaking hinge

galvanized cans,

smoking cheap cigars

and tossing the lids

You,

you are the ill society

that thrives upon the pain

and breathes the dying breath

from her chest.

You,

you possess the feet

that stamp her underneath

the dust of your machines

You,

you screaming individuality

not to be blamed for this

unholy sin

You,

you are the mass murderer

with your spinning blade

piercing her heart

only to make her bleed

You,

yes, you society

you and your slime

one of a kind

leaving her lifeless

of your own design

or the lack to do otherwise.

But,

the sun will rise upon the day

when

you, society

will feel decay,

to grope about

in the dirt

sand on your tongue,

she won't be there with water

or air.

Explaining Green:

Of course,

well……there is this stuff

which comes from the sky,

they call it rain.

It just plips and plops on the

grass, leaves and a few other

items,

Then,

a biochemical process takes place

and that blips and blops with an

end product called…..green.

We place our species

before the feet

of a carbon monoxide

improvement,

steaming forest gone

breathe deep

my dear chainsaw

smell our children's air

Four door Chevy

a painless down payment

on a double wide

fast marriage ceremony,

one in the oven,

children.

For a honeymoon,

heart shaped pool

in the Poconos,

that's my Tony

always so cool!

Pardon me dear

but would you mind

getting your tit's

out of my drink,

whiskey doesn't mix

with maternal instinct

Students stand in grey contempt

while computers stare

into another day's eye,

soon the trains arrive.

Within moments

the platform assumes

its cadaver profile,

the cars are gone

having finished an aluminum

suckling process

CHAPTER THREE

Vietnam

I raise my glass in toast

to the great department of

disability for their effort

helping 'my generation'.

I drink again

to all of the doctors and their

helpers,

designing new and improved limbs.

I slug this one

for the family

testing their love for 'him'.

The Vietnam Veteran

or

the part who made it home!

Vietnam

The taller mountains

and buildings

tore very small holes

in the mist

a seagull watched all of this.

The 'Harbor Princess'

more liken to a slave

carried the weary

to their working day.

Alcatraz

screamed with hate

from the pain of escape

such a cold morning

to meet San Francisco,

such a cold day

to meet the free world

Blessed are

the traditional fools

living in regret

a life spent

on one mistake.

Blessed are

the traditional children

acquired through gallantry

quartered with precision

by courtroom weekends,

for they

shall inherit the grief

This world means

busted bars

and broken dreams

sunny highways going

sunbeams coming my way

lonely faces

Christ-like renditions

of nothing

cash registers growling

those few

embarking

on a scheme

with broken dreams

following

those sunny highways

Its limp

cardboard soul lost

with arms and legs

torn off,

once he ate well

now,

hungry

sitting in a corner

next to a fire extinguisher

talking quietly

with a skid row cup

Eggs and Grits

buttered pickup trucks,

David Duke

sun-glassed mask

shot-gunned negros

in those old days.

Wallace walked with a limp

Bud provides the beer

for big belt buckles

trying to digest

carpet-bagging

Yankee opinion

Deep within the cavern

sounds become an echo

calling a monotonous hue,

the walls so chilled

I brush them more

with the depth,

water wipes my shirt

getting it wet.

Deeper I descend

until the air has weight

and the stalagmites

grin

I say hello

then ask directions

Societies violence

carefully outlined

in the early edition,

slowly dissolves

leaving ideas fused

to the concrete

next to the gum.

This city becomes

another holocaust,

wise men smoulder

in ignorant flames,

love lies dying

mostly in vain

Yesterday stands on her corner

rehearsing pornography

rattling a tin cup

laughing maliciously.

She is a rerun

a thief

of tomorrows dreams

stealing the donation

from behind your grin.

Yesterday sits on a bench

finding humor

in last week obits

she mourns no one

after today begins

I feel my being

roaming

Thursdays emotions,

kicking things

spilling sour memories

A slow rain

absorbs the sidewalk

chalked hopscotch

melting free,

patch work plans

make up another day.

Fantasies chase

monsters away

laser guns

rat tat tat

from young lips

all gone.

Crack invaded

the neighborhood

conquered and stayed,

the new rat tat tat

is a Glock nine

When you fall down

it is where you remain.

The address here

was always poor

kids were clean when they

walked to the store

but today

no one skips over crack

a half of clip will enter your head

a mother will know,

her baby is dead.

A slow rain

absorbs the sidewalk

chalked body outline

and blood

being washed to the curb.

It is so kind of Hugh

to lend me his girl,

quick bring the tape

so that we may dwell on her.

This magazine

with Teflon page's

and Pavlovian sensors

to measure the heat

of hopped up dreams

and pent up

subscription rates

Siagon girls

are cute

they have nice little legs

they are very understanding

after you pay

Vietnam entertainment.

Gentle ocean waves

repenting for last night's moon

sobered by the day

of prophetic Sun rays,

silent whispered waves

faint sounds they make

I listen from quiet sand,

gentle ocean waves

benign to my feelings

inside rage

all of the killing

drama in full array,

gentle ocean waves

washing the blood away

while your trigger finger stays,

Vietnam never goes away!

Bubbles climb

to the rim,

disappearing

into stagnant air,

joy leaves the wine

as dreams go flat

in your indifference,

such is the sour taste

of day old champagne

or a wife

neglected

for a billiard table

So I blow my eyebrows

about this rippled page,

thinking about a woman

pushing Dutch steak

around her restaurant plate.

The last supper

Christ must have felt like that

betrayed

by love

While the candle retires

I think of checkout counters

where wine, bread and cheese

go totally unnoticed,

only the cigarettes

pry a crowbar smile.

More wine

with an unnoticed label

I would be better off

as a carburetor

Such a meager plea

words of moisture

cool and fresh

yet filled with additives,

don't come to me

in your liquid limousine

speaking softly

only to conceal

the scream

CHAPTER FOUR

My eyeballs were sweating

when you left,

some say coffee will do that

I don't know.

The world seemed to collapse

but it didn't really,

people were starving

in Bangladesh

for food,

let alone love

Parents may only be

enslaved stone cutters,

working with crude tools

worn out from building

their own

decrepit tombs

Maybe the wind

will tell you things,

sweet breeze

and smiling white

your lips should have

such a treat,

maybe the wind

will kiss them for me

The ocean

sighs too vainly

with every manicured wave,

signing the sand

in mounds of silhouettes

casting translucent shadows

from the evening Sun

watching romantically,

the ocean is in love.

Winds

sing too quietly

with a cultured voice

begging breathlessly,

the wind is in love.

Could I make you a slave

of our common desire,

should I speak of love

or burnt offerings?

Love is illusive

clouded Summer skies

we sketch airless designs

gathered on the horizon,

I draw abstract things

and you feign understanding.

We talk of galleries

to hang our feelings in

who would come view

a composite such as ours?

an empty museum

closing its doors

hanging nothing that soars

Where have I wronged

what truth has been mislaid

what feelings have I sold

for this blown glass behavior?

What can be said

when there is nay a question

what good are answers

if no one wants to hear them?

I am an oblong wheel

an unfelt feeling

having no compassion

nothing to yield

Mothers protest

with wailing appeals,

drowning the sound

of warriors climbing

the steps

two soldiers in uniform,

one carries

the telegram

the other a death.

Love could produce

such useless things,

a clock without hours

calendars without days

feelings inflating a sense of identity.

Happiness could produce

joyful poverty

mad illusions of stability,

journeys to a rainbows end,

hours waiting for the ship to come in.

Love could produce

such useless things,

neglected children

outcast

marked and shunned

faulty rejections

of procreation

Don't ask for real love

in a Palm oil relationship,

sex doesn't donate a cent

toward real love.

During those midnight encounters

we are simply friends,

don't ask me where I've been

I also know of

lonely places

where they serve

non-dairy creamers

for lack of real love.

I have vivid recollections

of trite conversations

wearing fashions

and dripping mascara

from the corner of their eyes,

only pretending to cry

when I said go,

sure baby

I understand your position,

here in the missionary

it's called love

Summer

smell of fresh paint

burnt umbra bodies

sizzling on the bench,

orange horizons

bug infested nights

citronella candles

and swing set encounters

under yellow

porch lights

I am nothing without Teresa, this is for

you my dear....

Melba dear

I ain't much at woids,

but I likes ya very much

because I do.

Melba honey,

I tink about ya

when I'm drivin my truck

and I knows I love ya

cause I don't stop for no coffee

an I don't look at no goils,

I mus have rocks in me head

Is Max Factor

in every bedroom,

sweet perfumed hair

moist tasty lips

even your douche

is peppermint.

Who thinks of love

with an applicator

heartless gauze pad

or latex radar dish,

women have become

stock options

in both Hershey

and the Mars

corporation

CHAPTER FIVE

City Lights watch the lonely

joy goes un-noticed,

sidewalks sit in silent longing

for just a few footsteps.

Patrol cars sneak around corners

Chevrolet grilles smile

sarcastically,

wish you were here

I'm having a wonderful time.

Broken pockets

went dry days ago

billboard signs

telephone poles

they all hurt your shoulders,

the park bench is always wet,

wish you were here

I have to borrow a stamp

Like a wedge

we spread apart

with every

sledge-hammer blow

weekend.

More fibers are lost

separated into chips

of cruel memories

was this love

a proud tall tree

reduced to kindling

To forge happiness

with such crude tools,

an apathetic god

a human race without mores

battling doubt

while moving mountains

with the hope

of a better view.

And what is self?

an empty shell

and what brings meaning

into this massive turmoil?

You my love

You

Love may fill

your cadaver dreams

though other vessels

are quickly built

to allow words to pass

between two sheets

of all self-doubt

our security lites

in a different way,

trying to stand with

all its weight

on one leg

I drift to a drink

from a grey metallic spring

a radio shouts

the taste of chlorine

Please Margaret Mead

give me a feeling

of respect for clothing

that leaves nothing

for the imagination.

I approached

National Geographic

but they only subscribe

to the sex life of bugs and rocks

that like to hide.

Sigmund Freud

better tell me the correct

edification

when a woman

with cigars,

blows smoke in my face

and kisses her female companion

Within one life span

may exist

enough true rest

to occupy

all airport furniture

that ever did exist

hard chrome corners

a vinyl edge

without any thought for comfort,

fatigue assumes wheels

one war

and to many doctors,

parking me on the end,

they always say

I will be back

After I gave him the fin!

Very depressing

the puke green

and stainless steel

with limp fried

potatoes,

excitement came from

Vanna

turning letters

in high heels

garbled top forty

scrubbed and pressed

playboys

all dressed without

permission to go

Any windy morning

can blow through

the hole

you once occupied,

one to many

promises

I'll quit tomorrow

etched

on yellow flesh,

English Leather

distilled from the dregs

trying to cover the smell

or lack of intelligence,

that went somewhere

without common sense

We accept Christ

because he died on the cross

and the people

from Reader's Digest saw it.

We read about his exploits

in special magazines marked

miscellaneous without the centerfold.

Securely we sit

looking through the iron bars of our

drugstore eyeglasses accepting pain

and death for another reward.

A bowl of salty water and Tokay wine

paper thin wafers and passing signs

file in solemn ranks quiet and chaste

while guys in cockroach hats

all agree with one book

and destroy the others.

Using a blatant stare

on a 12 inch woofer

she looks like

Degas doodled her,

on his check

for Absinthe

Vincent came in

he didn't notice me

I moved my palette

to another table,

the quartet went on break

she just sat there

the poor bitch

could not hear

Don't tell me of her

wine glass eyes

concentrate on her

nouveau riche grin

and tell me of her

sparkling alibis

and apathetic expressions,

now

may I pour

your 3 dollar champagne

My head becomes a top

spun by some Italian

who dreams of recipes

handed down to him

with his grapes,

are these innocent things

and my thirst a sin

only to repent

and be spun around again

until I retch

My personality

should never

guard a king,

my feelings

should never

find an

empty sea,

my confusion

should never

travel in space,

my life

should always

avoid the press

Oh how I squirm

in my manhood

when you say

you're late,

like a woolen sweater

I itch and scratch

for escape,

only to be relieved

by a period

with so much

at stake

Artist and poets

commit suicide

while philosophers

and Generals

sign up for Medicare,

who gave thought

such a brilliant sense

of humor

My stale cigarette pulls

on a rising headache

the beer warms up

another non-stop tendency,

yet I dread the thought

of dialing that number

for misery,

my mind copulates

with creative things

leaving them all

un-satisfied,

so its time to get up

and pull up my fly

only to hear my name

pronounced,

frustration

Why is life

a boycott dream

restricted from sight

by a blind overseer,

and who builds statues

of empty heroes

but those pursuing

that secret mirror

ACKNOWLEDGEMENTS

Undoubtedly the best way to begin a page of this nature would be to thank the population of the Earth, because this material provides the aggregate from which all poetry is composed. Though it would be more direct to say that the entire team here at Alchemy Studio, LLc should win those honors. Teresa has to put up with me, not an easy task, and then there are the people at the buttons, Sloan, Kathleen, Brendan, Kathy being the main players who receive thank you cards. Please add a number of professionals whose work is appreciated to make all of the loose parts fit together into this book you have in your hand. At times it seems my contributions are but insignificant tirades, bound securely between two covers always saying thank you!

CHAPTER ONE

CHAPTER TWO

CHAPTER THREE

CHAPTER FOUR

CHAPTER FIVE

About the Author

Born the son of a struggling coal miner
and a well-educated mother in the anthracite
region of Pennsylvania, Jason learned early how
to work and fight for his every success. Travels
began as a young man with the Mekong Delta of
South Vietnam. He lived and worked in the
Caribbean, Australia, Europe, and throughout the
United States. Jason lives what he writes about,
looking at the big picture with a microscope,
then providing a raw commentary on the view.

www.ingramcontent.com/pod-product-compliance
Lightning Source LLC
Chambersburg PA
CBHW071007040426
42443CB00007B/698

9 780615 806587